MUHAMMAD ALI

ARLENE SCHULMAN

In Consultation with Martha Cosgrove,
M.A. and Reading Specialist

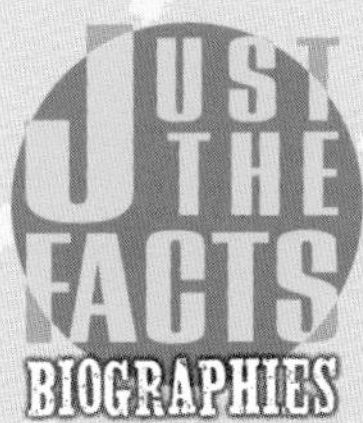

LERNER PUBLICATIONS COMPANY / MINNEAPOLIS

Martha Cosgrove has a master's degree from the University of Minnesota in secondary education, with an emphasis on developmental and remedial reading. She is licensed in 7–12 English and language arts, developmental reading, and remedial reading. She has had several works published, and she gives numerous state and national presentations in her areas of expertise.

Lerner Publications Company
A division of Lerner Publishing Group
241 First Avenue North
Minneapolis, Minnesota U.S.A.

Website address: www.lernerbooks.com

Library of Congress Cataloging-in-Publication Data

Schulman, Arlene.
Muhammad Ali / by Arlene Schulman.
p. cm. – (Just the facts biographies)
Includes bibliographical references and index.
ISBN: 0-8225-2448-1 (lib. bdg. : alk. paper)
1. Ali, Muhammad, 1942- –Juvenile literature. 2. Boxers (Sports)–United States–Biography–Juvenile literature. I. Title. II. Series.
GV1132.A44S367 2005
796.83'092–dc22 2004028219

Manufactured in the United States of America
1 2 3 4 5 6 - JR - 10 09 08 07 06 05

Contents

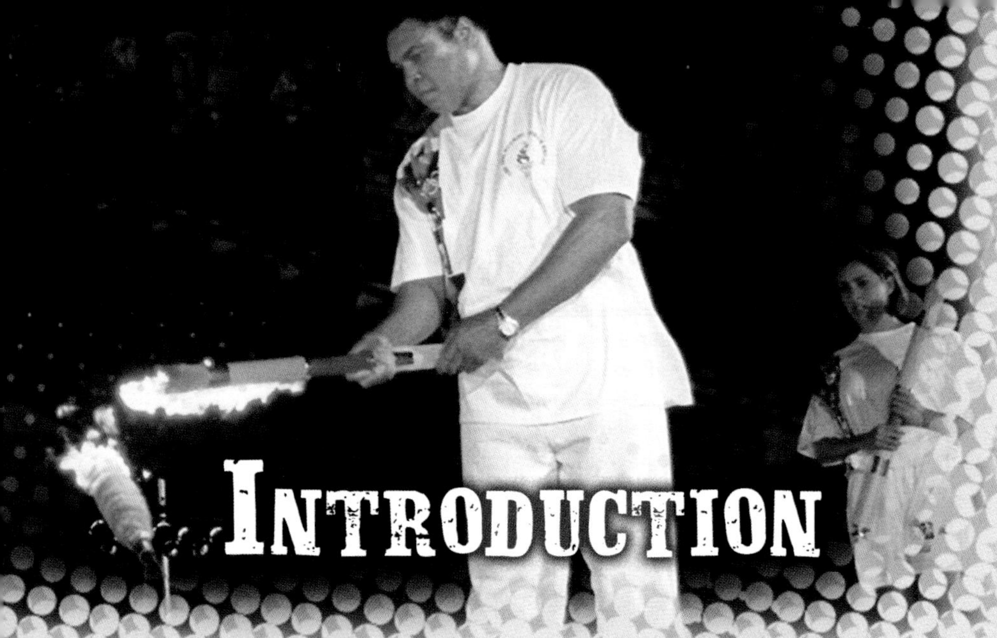

Introduction

(*Above*) **Ali lights the Olympic flame for the 1996 Summer Olympic Games in Atlanta, Georgia. U.S. swimmer Janet Evans looks on.**

On the evening of July 19, 1996, the crowd in Atlanta, Georgia, was pumped and excited. The Summer Olympics were about to open. The stadium had grown dark as the opening ceremonies started. Everyone was waiting for the Olympic torch to enter the stadium. The lighting of the Olympic flame signaled the official opening of the Games. The honor of lighting the torch usually went to someone who'd been an Olympic athlete and who meant something special to the country hosting the Games.

As the crowd watched, a small, slight runner carried the torch into the stadium. The crowd recognized the runner as Janet Evans, an American swimmer. She had won medals and had set records in the last two Summer Olympics. But to whom was she carrying the torch? Who was going to light the flame? As Janet made her way slowly around the track, a man dressed in white waited for her. He was tall and strong. As Janet got nearer, the crowd roared. They could see who'd be lighting the torch at the Games–Muhammad Ali!

Janet met up with Ali, who reached carefully for the torch. He raised the torch skyward for all to see. Then he leaned down to light a wire that would send the flame upward to a large bowl. The flame went higher and higher, until it reached the bowl and caught fire. The 1996 Summer Olympic Games could now start.

Ali, born Cassius Clay, had come a long way from his childhood days. Sitting with his mother at night, he'd tell her that one day he was going to be the boxing champion of the world. In their small house in Louisville, Kentucky, when the sun had set and the lights were out, twelve-year-old Cassius would describe the scene to his mother. He would knock out opponents one by one. His hands would be raised in victory, as the announcer introduced him as the new world champion.

CHAPTER 1
DREAMS OF GLORY

(Above) **Clay's hometown of Louisville, Kentucky, in the 1940s**

CASSIUS MARCELLUS CLAY JR. was born to Odessa and Cassius Clay Sr. on January 17, 1942, in Louisville, Kentucky. (He would later have a younger brother, named Rudy.) Cassius Jr. demanded attention at a very early age. The story goes that, soon after giving birth to Cassius, Mrs. Clay could hear her young son's cries. His screams soon woke up the other babies in the hospital.

"Gee-gee, gee-gee," were Cassius's first words, his mother said. He later claimed that he was trying to say Golden Gloves. This referred to a famous national boxing contest. "When he was a child, he never sat still," his mother recalled. "He walked and talked . . . before his time."

It's a Fact!

Each state has its own Golden Gloves competition. State winners then go on to compete in the national competition, called the Golden Gloves Tournament of Champions.

Early Life

In the 1940s in Louisville, African Americans lived in separate neighborhoods from whites. Black people were allowed to sit only in the back rows of buses and movie theaters. Most stores and restaurants wouldn't serve African Americans. Black children and white children could not go to school together. This system of separating blacks and whites was called segregation. States of the southern United States, including Kentucky, followed segregated ways. Some southern states had made segregation the law.

In the South when Clay was a boy, drinking fountains were segregated by law.

Louisville had three African American neighborhoods–East End, the California area, and West End, where the Clays lived. Like most families in the neighborhood, they were poor. The family car was at least ten years old with worn-out tires. The house always needed painting. The front porch sagged. During rainy weather, water leaked through the roof and walls. Cassius and Rudy's clothes had been handed down from someone else. Once in a while, but not often, the Clays were able to afford a new shirt or a new pair of pants for Cassius and Rudy.

Odessa Clay worked when her sons were young. She cleaned houses and cared for the children of well-to-do white families. She earned four dollars a day. Odessa was a religious woman.

On Sundays, she and her two sons attended Mount Zion Baptist Church, where Cassius sang in the choir. She taught Cassius to always treat people with kindness and respect.

Cassius Sr. was stern, and his sons both loved and feared him. Cassius Sr. painted billboards and signs for a living. Almost every Baptist church in Louisville owned one of his religious murals (wall paintings). Although he taught Cassius and Rudy to paint signs, he didn't want them to become sign painters. He wanted them to become doctors or lawyers. African American sign painters in Louisville in the 1940s and 1950s didn't make much money.

The Clays were a close-knit family with a troubled side. When Cassius Sr. had too much alcohol to drink, he became violent. Odessa Clay called the police several times seeking protection from her husband. He was arrested for driving recklessly and for other violent behavior.

Finding Boxing

In 1954, when Cassius was twelve, his father bought him a brand-new bicycle for Christmas. The family was poor, so getting a new bike was a big deal.

Young Cassius proudly pedaled his new bike throughout West End. One day, he rode with a friend to a large marketplace at the Columbia Auditorium in Louisville. The two boys parked their bicycles outside. They looked at furniture, crafts, and other goods and munched on free hot dogs, popcorn, and candy. When they left the show, Cassius couldn't find his bicycle. It had been stolen.

Joe Martin, a police officer and amateur boxing coach, was teaching boxing in the auditorium's basement gym. Someone suggested that Cassius report the stolen bicycle to Martin. Cassius ran up to the police officer and told him angrily that he'd beat up the kid who'd taken his bike. Martin suggested that, if Cassius wanted to beat up somebody, he'd better learn how to box.

When Cassius looked around the gym, he almost forgot about his missing bike. Boys were boxing each other and skipping rope. He could hear the rat-tat-tat of the punches to the speed bag and the hard, thudding punches to the heavy bag. The air smelled like sweat. Joe Martin invited the excited Cassius to join his boxing club. He sent him home with an application form for his parents to fill out.

The future champ at the age of twelve

A few days later, Cassius noticed Joe Martin coaching amateur boxers on a TV show called *Tomorrow's Champions.* Cassius decided that he would join Martin's gym. He got his parents to agree.

Cassius was thin and didn't have much muscle. He weighed only eighty-nine pounds. Although he'd never put on boxing gloves before, he went to the gym every day. "He stood out because, I guess, he had more determination than most boys," Martin said, "and he had the speed to get him someplace." Cassius learned how to throw punches. He practiced by hitting the heavy bag and the speed bag. He improved his quickness by jumping rope. Soon he could throw punches like a professional.

It's a Fact!

From the beginning, Cassius was known for his quickness. To keep improving, Cassius had Rudy throw rocks at him. Cassius dodged every one.

Cassius spent almost all of his spare time in the gym. He didn't lose his confidence when he was hit. His feet moved as quickly as his hands. After a fight, he would pretend to announce over the loudspeaker: "Ladies and gentlemen, introducing the new world champion. . . ."

First Success

Six weeks after his first visit to Joe Martin's gym, thirteen-year-old Cassius was scheduled to appear on *Tomorrow's Champions.* He knocked on the doors of his neighbors' houses to tell them that he was going to fight on television. On the day of the show, he stepped into the ring against a boy from one of Louisville's white neighborhoods. Cassius was nervous, but he punched and ducked for three two-minute rounds. (A round is a time period in a boxing match.) Judges kept track of how often the fighters had connected, or successfully hit, the opponent. The bell rang to signal the end of the fight. The judges added up their scorecards. The winner was Cassius Clay!

Young Cassius was blessed with fast feet and faster hands, and he learned quickly. He was the first one to arrive at the gym and the last one to leave. Joe Martin later recalled that Cassius was a natural. He was fast and moved well with the gloves on, despite having no previous training.

Boxing Rules

All amateur fights last for either three three-minute rounds or five two-minute rounds. In amateur fights, five judges award points to each fighter based on performance. (Professional fights have three judges.)

The person with the most points at the end of the match wins. This type of victory is called winning by decision. When all the judges agree, the winner wins by unanimous decision. If the judges don't all agree, the winner wins by a split decision. If the judges can't decide on a winner, the fight is a draw.

The winner can also be determined more quickly. This can happen if one opponent is knocked out. The referee—the official who stands in the ring—can also stop a fight if the referee believes an opponent is too hurt or tired to continue.

Cassius grew more confident after his first victory. His friends and family gave him a lot of support. But West End could be a tough neighborhood. Cassius and his friends had long avoided a bully who picked on the kids. Then, after his boxing success, Cassius challenged the bully to a fight. Cassius threw a few punches, and the bully ran home with a bloody nose. Cassius became known as the "King."

In 1955, Cassius was going to DuValle Junior High School. Training and traveling to boxing tournaments with Joe Martin kept him busy after school. "There wasn't nothing to do in the streets. The kids would throw rocks and stand under the street lights," he later said about his childhood. "[There] wasn't nothing else to do [but] boxing."

It's a Fact!

Besides boxing, Cassius loved horse racing. Sometimes, he'd wake up early to watch the horses train at Churchill Downs, a famous racetrack in Louisville. He loved the stables and the sleek, muscular horses. He would race alongside them as they sped by during their practice runs.

The King worked out every morning. He'd wake up at 4:00 A.M., run for two hours, go home and sleep, and arrive at DuValle Junior High at 9:00. Sometimes he and Rudy raced the bus for twenty blocks to school. The children on the bus laughed at them. Cassius told people he was running to get in fighting shape.

In 1956, when he started going to Louisville's Central High School, Cassius was bragging that he was the toughest kid in town. He ate a healthful diet. He never drank alcohol or smoked cigarettes. He entered state and national Golden Gloves tournaments. By 1960, he had won six Kentucky Golden Gloves tournaments and two national Golden Gloves championships. In 1959 and 1960, he won two national Amateur Athletic Union (AAU) titles.

Around boys, he was always goofing off, joking, and pretending to box in the halls. Around girls, he was polite and shy. During his senior year, he dated Mildred Davis. One day, Cassius let Mildred wear a necklace that had a little gold glove on a gold chain. The necklace was part of his prize for winning the national Golden Gloves championships in Chicago, Illinois.

Cassius didn't pay much attention in class, and he didn't spend much time on homework. Instead, he went to the gym. "I saw there was no future in getting a high school education or even a college education," Cassius later said.

Cassius graduated from Central High with a D-minus grade point average. Some teachers thought Cassius shouldn't be allowed to graduate because of his poor grades. But principal Atwood Wilson was behind Cassius. "Why, in one night, he'll make more money than the principal and all you teachers make in a year," Wilson said. "If every teacher here fails him, he's still not going to fail." On June 11, 1960, Cassius received his high school diploma. His classmates stood up and cheered for him. He could go after his boxing goals full-time.

"I started boxing because I thought this was the fastest way for a black person to make it in this country. I was not that bright and quick in school, couldn't be a football or a basketball player 'cause you have to go to college and get all kinds of degrees and pass examinations," he said. "A boxer can just go to the gym, jump around, turn professional, win a fight, get a break, and he is in the ring. If he's good enough he makes more money than ballplayers make all their lives."

CHAPTER 2 STING LIKE A BEE

IN 1960, by the time Cassius was eighteen, he had won 100 out of 108 amateur fights. But amateurs don't get prize money. Cassius wanted to turn professional, or pro. He wanted to earn money and start making a name for himself.

Joe Martin convinced Cassius to stay an amateur so he could try out for the U.S. Olympic team instead. (At that time, only amateurs could compete in the Olympics.) Martin explained that in boxing, the Olympic champion and the top-ranked pro are at the same level. Cassius earned a spot on the team.

***(Above)* At the age of eighteen, Clay had already won many fights. He felt ready to take on the world.**

The Story of the Olympic Games

More than 2,700 years ago—in 776 B.C.—ancient Greeks held the first Olympic Games. The Greeks lived along the Mediterranean Sea. At that long-ago time, the cities of ancient Greece were often battling one another for power. But every four years, they stopped all their battles for a while and sent their best athletes to Olympia, a valley in southwestern Greece.

The Greeks held a religious festival in Olympia. The festival featured events of athletic strength and skill. The oldest event at the Olympia festival, or Olympic Games, was a footrace. The Greeks later added boxing, wrestling, discus throwing, and javelin throwing to the Olympics. Winners were admired throughout Greece.

About 2,200 years ago—in 197 B.C.—the Romans conquered the Greeks. The Romans lived in the center of the Mediterranean region, and they let the Games go on. Athletes from all over the Mediterranean region began competing. But about 1,600 years ago—in A.D. 394—the Roman emperor Theodosius stopped the Olympic Games. He was a Christian. He banned the Games because they were part of a religious festival that wasn't Christian.

But in the late 1800s, a wealthy Frenchman named Baron Pierre de Coubertin brought back the ancient Games. Coubertin believed that the new, modern Olympics would be a way for the different countries of the world to compete peacefully on the athletic field. He wanted the world to have a different way to fight than on a battlefield. The first modern Olympics were held in Athens, the capital of Greece, in 1896. These first modern Olympic Games were Summer Games. The first Winter Olympic Games took place in 1924 in Chamonix, France.

1960 Olympics

The 1960 Olympics were held in Rome, Italy. Enthusiastic and outgoing, Cassius Clay became the most popular athlete at the Games. He waved and said hello to everyone he met. He shook hands, signed autographs, and gave interviews.

He was introduced to Floyd Patterson, the world heavyweight champion and a former Olympic gold medalist. Cassius said that, sometime in the future, the two fighters would meet for the heavyweight title. "So long, Floyd, be seeing you–in about two years–when I whip you for your title," he told Patterson.

In Olympic competition, a heavyweight boxer has to weigh at least 179 pounds. Cassius didn't weigh this much, so he competed as a light heavyweight at 178 pounds. He beat three opponents easily to qualify for the finals. In the fight for the gold medal, he beat Zbigniew Pietrzykowski of Poland.

After the fight, he didn't want to take off his gold medal, even at night. "I didn't sleep too good because I had to sleep on my back so the medal wouldn't cut me," he recalled. "But I didn't care. I was the Olympic champ." Back

The U.S. Olympic boxing team in Rome. Clay *(far right)* competed as a light heavyweight.

home, his father painted the front porch steps red, white, and blue.

After the Olympics

On the way back from Rome, Cassius stopped in New York City as part of the Olympic celebration. Many people had seen Cassius win the gold medal on television. Tourists recognized him and asked for his autograph. He introduced himself as Cassius Clay, the great fighter.

Back in Louisville, the town turned out for a giant parade. The returning hero waved to the crowds from the back of a pink Cadillac. Cassius later admitted that he liked all the attention–both from the crowds and the media.

IT'S A FACT!

While in New York, Cassius met Sugar Ray Robinson, a famous boxing champion. He owned a restaurant in the city. Cassius asked Sugar Ray to be his manager. But Robinson was still fighting and wasn't interested in working with the younger fighter.

But not everything was easy. Cassius had represented the United States in the Olympics and had won the gold medal. But in the United States, he was still a black man who didn't get all the same rights as a white man. This unfair treatment of African Americans is a form of racial discrimination.

A famous story says that in Louisville, Cassius and a friend stopped in a restaurant for a hamburger. But the owner of the restaurant wouldn't serve African Americans. Outside the restaurant, a white motorcycle gang leader demanded that Cassius hand over his gold medal. A fight broke out.

Afterward, Cassius became disgusted with the way that he and other African Americans were treated in the United States. The story goes that he threw his precious gold medal into the Ohio River, which flows through Louisville. After the Olympics, Cassius began to speak publicly against racial discrimination in the United States.

Turning Pro

Cassius had many offers to turn professional after the Olympics. But he needed managers to set up fights. He chose the Louisville Sponsoring Group, which was made up of eleven wealthy, white businessmen. The group would choose Cassius's opponents and set up fights. The businessmen would negotiate, or discuss the money he'd be paid, for radio and television broadcasts of his fights.

Cassius's first goals were to buy a house for his parents and a brand-new red Cadillac for himself. The Louisville Group's first goal was to find a trainer for Cassius. The group wanted someone who would polish his skills and teach him how to box as a professional.

Boxing Terms

bout: a boxing match

corner: any of the angles of a boxing ring. During a bout, boxing opponents stay in opposite corners between rounds. The other two corners are neutral.

counterpunch: to hit into the unguarded area an opponent leaves open after he or she punches

duck: to move under a punch

footwork: the active way a boxer moves with the feet during a bout. Good footwork allows a fighter to be in position to throw or avoid punches.

heavy bag: a large hanging or fixed punching bag that boxers use to practice their punches. Typically, boxers "work the bag" in rounds.

hook: a short power punch thrown with a hooked arm

jab: a quick, straight punch thrown from the chin with the leading hand

one-two: the combination of a jab and a straight right

one-two-three: the combination of a jab, a straight right, and a left hook

power punch: a punch that's delivered with the force of the legs and the upper body

round: a time period that makes up a section of a fight

speed bag: a small bag hung slightly above a boxer, who hits it with short, quick punches. Training on the speed bag builds stamina and improves timing.

straight right: a power punch thrown with a straight right hand

uppercut: a power punch thrown up from the waist

Cassius eventually teamed up with Angelo Dundee, the trainer of seven boxing champions. Dundee saw something special in Cassius from the very beginning. Later Dundee claimed to have even taught young Cassius how to punch with more snap. (Cassius disagreed with with Dundee's statement.)

Cassius moved to Miami, Florida, where Dundee trained his fighters. Cassius lived in a one-room apartment in a rough neighborhood. He trained at Miami's Fifth Street Gym. The floor sagged, and the windows were dirty. The gym was decorated with fight posters and old photographs. People paid fifty cents to watch the fighters work out.

Cassius enjoyed living on his own and visiting the music clubs around Miami. He liked seeing the African American musicians of the time. These people included Fats Domino, Little Richard, Sam Cooke, and Chubby Checker. But he tried to stay focused on his goals. Even though the city offered lots of distractions, Cassius didn't give in. He stuck to his training, because he saw his dedication as the way to reach success. "The hardest part of the training is the loneliness," he admitted in a quiet moment.

Clay liked to sing almost as much as he liked to talk.

Just as in Louisville, Cassius was always the first one at the gym and the last one to leave. He would fight anyone. Angelo Dundee was impressed by his dedication and his natural skill.

Cassius had his first fight, or bout, as a professional in October 1960. He faced Tunney Hunsaker at the Louisville Convention Center.

Hunsaker was not highly rated. Most people thought Clay was likely to beat him. Clay outdanced and outboxed Hunsaker, winning in the sixth round. All three judges gave Clay the highest score. He received two thousand dollars in prize money.

Hunsaker was impressed by how fast Ali could move. Hunsaker had tried everything he knew to beat Ali, but Ali never wavered. Ali would soon be world champion, Hunsaker predicted.

IT'S A FACT!

The number of rounds in a professional fight varies. Beginners' matches are usually four rounds. When Clay started his career, the championship fights were fifteen rounds. To cut down on injuries, championship fights became twelve rounds in the 1980s.

A Winning Streak

Clay won his next fourteen bouts. And he started to attract national attention. He gave interviews, where he sang poetry that rhymed. Usually, the rhymes warned or poked fun of his opponents. Reporters from newspapers, radio, and television loved Clay. He was handsome and colorful. He always gave them interesting quotes.

He loved the camera, and the camera loved him. Photographers admired his expressive face. Women fell for him, one after another. Even with his outgoing personality, his rhymes, jokes, and boasts, Cassius had a quiet side. In private, when the reporters had left the room, he often became shy and thoughtful.

At the end of 1962, he faced his biggest test. Forty-nine-year-old Archie Moore, the former light heavyweight champion, was to be his challenger. Clay was twenty years old and favored to win. Clay had fought only fifteen pro fights. Moore had fought more than two hundred.

The fight would be Clay's first bout against a big-name opponent. He sang this rhyme at press conferences before the fight.

When you come to the fight
Don't block the aisles
and don't block the door
'cuz Archie Moore will fall in four.

Clay was six feet three inches tall and weighed a trim 204 pounds. Moore, who was shorter, was

It's a Fact!

All professional boxers are required to wear a mouthpiece during a bout. No round can start without the boxers wearing their mouthpieces. And a fighter can lose points by spitting out the mouthpiece during a round.

overweight at 197 pounds. The bell rang to begin the fight. Moore stood with his arms crossed to protect his jaw and his chin. Clay started punching and wore him down. In the fourth round, Clay hit Moore with a right jab, and Moore lost his mouthpiece. With a combination of punches, Clay sent Moore to the floor. Moore managed to get up, only to be knocked down again. He got up again and went down for the third and final time. Clay knocked him out, as predicted, in the fourth round. Clay was too young, too fast, and too big for him. It was Moore's last fight.

Seven of Clay's eight fights had ended in the round that he had predicted. He became even more popular with the press and the fans. In early 1963, he was scheduled to fight Doug Jones at New York's Madison Square Garden. "Jones likes to mix. So I'll let it go six," he predicted. He

Archie Moore *(left)* buckles under Clay's punches in a 1962 fight.

promoted himself on *The Tonight Show.* The guests on this late-night TV program usually were actors or singers, not boxers. Madison Square Garden was sold out for a professional fight for the first time in ten years.

But this matchup turned out to be one of the worst fights of Clay's career. It didn't end in six. It went to ten rounds. After so much publicity, the fight wasn't a great bout. Jones performed at his best, and the fight ended in a ten-round decision in favor of Clay. An unimpressed crowd threw trash, program books, bottles, and peanuts into the ring. Clay said later how much he'd underestimated Jones.

Just after the fight, Clay met a man named Bundini Brown. He seemed to be able to motivate Clay. Brown became a close friend, who could push him in training and through fights. Brown also helped Clay with his poetry.

Clay rode around in his Cadillac, listening to music with friends. He didn't train very hard for his next opponent, former British heavyweight champion Henry Cooper. At the fight in London, England, held on June 18, 1963, he entered the ring in a red robe with "Cassius the Greatest" written on the back. Although he eventually knocked out Cooper, Clay was knocked down for the first time in his career. He was back on his feet quickly. "I am the greatest!" he shouted after the referee stopped the fight.

Fighting Sonny

In his twentieth professional bout, Clay faced Sonny Liston for the heavyweight title. When Clay began his career, the heavyweight champion of the world was the one and only heavyweight champion. (In later years, the title would be awarded to various fighters by several different groups.) The fight against Liston would give Clay the chance to prove that he was the greatest boxer in the world.

Sonny Liston was 220 pounds of solid muscle. He rarely smiled or showed any expression in his face. With his fast left hook, he was considered unbeatable. He had turned pro in 1953, when he was twenty. He had won thirty-four bouts and had lost just one before he met Floyd Patterson for the heavyweight title in 1962. He had knocked out Patterson in the first round to claim the championship.

Lots of Titles

Since the 1960s, different professional groups—such as the World Boxing Council, the World Boxing Association, and the International Boxing Federation—have awarded world heavyweight boxing titles. So several fighters can hold the title at the same time. In Clay's time, however, only one boxing title existed.

The Liston-Clay heavyweight championship fight was to be held on February 25, 1964. Clay trained at the Fifth Street Gym in Miami. Even the Beatles, who were in Miami Beach to begin a concert tour, stopped by and posed with him for photographs. The pictures showed Clay playfully pretending to knock out the famous rock-and-roll musicians.

Before a fight, each fighter gets on a scale and publicly weighs in. The weigh-in before a

Clay takes out the Beatles *(left to right)*—Paul, John, Ringo, and George—with one blow.

fight is usually a quiet affair. But at this one, held the day before the fight at the Miami Convention Center, Clay stormed around in a carefully rehearsed show. He was waving his hands wildly and shouting at Liston, "Float like a butterfly, sting like a bee. We're ready to rumble, you big ugly bear! Let's get it on right now!"

IT'S A FACT!

Bundini Brown came up with the famous saying, "Float like a butterfly, sting like a bee." It referred to Clay's quick footwork and powerful punches.

The doctor assigned to check the fighters before the bout said that Clay was "emotionally unbalanced, scared to death and [likely] to crack up before he enters the ring." Some reporters believed this view. Others took Clay's performance for the act that it was. Headlines called him, "The Louisville Lip" and "The Mighty Mouth."

Clay was not expected to win. He entered the ring first, wearing a white, hooded robe that read "The Lip." When the fight began, Liston was slow and plodding. Clay was the opposite–fast with jabs and quick on his feet. He carried his hands low. He leaned back on the ropes that surround the ring to stay away from punches.

Liston's punches kept missing. In the third round, Clay cut him on the left side of his face. Liston had fought forty times before this matchup, and he had never once been cut. Liston returned to his corner, and his staff treated the cut with a medicine that would stop the bleeding. Somehow, when Liston pushed his gloves into Clay's face, the medication got into Clay's eyes. The burning in his eyes made it hard for Clay to see.

Clay tried to wipe the medication out of his eyes with his gloves. He swung wildly. After the end of the round, Clay sat down on his stool. He shouted to Angelo Dundee, "Cut my gloves off! I can't see!"

Dundee refused, flushing Clay's eyes with water and pushing him off his stool. Liston was still a blur, and Clay blindly ducked out of the way of his punches. When his eyes finally cleared in the sixth round, Clay began pushing Liston's head back with his fists. Bundini Brown shouted encouragement from outside the ring.

Liston was exhausted and battered. Before the bell rang for the start of the seventh round, he shook his head wearily and slumped on his stool.

Sonny Liston *(left)* can't hit the moving target in this 1964 fight with Clay.

He quit, too tired to continue. Cassius Clay was the new heavyweight champion. "I am king!" he shouted. "I am the greatest! I shook up the world!"

At the press conference afterward, he silenced the crowd of reporters. He demanded: "Who's the greatest?" There was no answer.

"Who's the greatest?" he asked again.

"You are," the crowd responded.

"Well, all right!" he said, satisfied.

Chapter 3 Don't Call Me Cassius

(*Above*) Clay became famous for his remarks outside the boxing ring.

In the 1960s, many African American athletes chose to be silent on civil rights (the struggle for equal rights). They focused on their sports, not on politics. But Cassius Clay would not be silent. He demanded to be given the same rights as any other American. "I went all the way to Italy to represent my country, won a gold medal, and now I come back to America and can't even get served at a five-and-dime store."

On other occasions, Clay talked about how many African Americans didn't feel free in America. He explained how hard it is to grow up in the ghetto, where success and intelligence don't mean as much as the ability to fight and be tough.

Joining the Nation of Islam

At the same time, most people didn't know that Clay had been attending meetings of the Nation of Islam. This is an African American religious group, not a country. The Nation of Islam practices a version of Islam, an ancient faith that came from the Middle East. Followers of Islam are called Muslims. They pray to Allah (God). Followers of the Nation of Islam are called Black Muslims. The leader of the Nation of Islam in the 1960s was Elijah Muhammad. His main spokesperson was Malcolm X.

Nation of Islam leaders believed that blacks and whites should remain separate or segregated. They believed that the African American population should form a separate nation within the United States. Many Black Muslims thought of white people as the devil. At the same time, however, African American and white civil rights leaders were working to end segregation in schools, restaurants, buses, hotels, and neighborhoods. They strongly disagreed with the goals of the Nation of Islam.

Cassius first learned about the Nation of Islam at the Rome Olympics in 1960. He had read a copy of the group's newspaper, *Muhammad Speaks*.

Elijah Muhammad

Elijah Muhammad's original name was Elijah Poole. He was born around October 7, 1897, in a rural part of Georgia. Elijah was one of twelve children born to William and Marie Poole. His father was a minister.

In 1919, Elijah married Clara Evans, with whom he had eight children. At the time of his marriage, Elijah worked for the railroad and for a brick company. But in April 1923, he took his family northward to Detroit, Michigan. There he got a job working on an automobile assembly line.

In 1930, Elijah met Wallace D. Fard, the founder of the Nation of Islam. Wallace Fard preached that it was time for African Americans to return to Islam, which he viewed as the religion of their ancient ancestors. When Elijah met him, Fard was selling silk products door-to-door. However, he said he was a prophet who came from Africa to help African Americans understand their history and their place in the world. According to Fard, the black race was the superior "original race." And African Americans were Islam's lost sheep. His job was to herd the sheep and bring them back home.

Elijah became Fard's main assistant and devoted follower. Fard gave Elijah the Muslim name Muhammad. (Muhammad is the Prophet of the ancient religion of Islam.) Fard disappeared on February 26, 1934. To this day, no one knows what happened to him. After his disappearance, Elijah took control of the Nation of Islam.

Then he began reading *Muhammad Speaks* regularly. Malcolm X visited him often at the Fifth Street Gym. For three years before the fight with Sonny Liston, Cassius and his brother Rudy snuck into Nation of Islam meetings at a Muslim temple in Miami. Clay didn't want to be noticed. He was afraid that, if people knew he was attending Nation of Islam meetings, he'd no longer be allowed to box.

IT'S A FACT!

Death threats had reached Clay before the Liston fight. Clay was worried. To calm himself, Clay and Malcolm X prayed together before Clay entered the ring.

Reporters suspected that Clay had joined the Nation of Islam. But it wasn't until a press conference after the title fight with Liston that he formally announced his membership in the group.

"People brand us as a hate group," he said. "They say we want to take over the country. . . . That is not true. Followers of Allah are the sweetest people in the world. . . . All they want to do is live in peace. . . . You can't condemn a man for wanting peace."

Clay also announced that he had changed his name to Muhammad Ali, which means "worthy of praise." Ali's great-grandfather, a slave, had taken the name Clay from his owner. Ali told reporters, "Don't call me by my slave name no more.

"I chose to be a Muslim," he continued. "I chose to be a follower of Elijah Muhammad because he was the only one offering definite plans which helped my people." Many people felt that Ali's decision to join the Nation of Islam had ruined his Olympic image. "I don't have to be what you want me to be," he retorted. "I'm free to be who I want."

Ali and the Nation of Islam

The Nation of Islam had a lot of influence on Muhammad Ali's life and career. Shortly after Ali's announcement, Herbert Muhammad, the son of Elijah Muhammad, became Ali's new manager. Eventually, Ali cut all ties with the Louisville Sponsoring Group.

Bundini Brown refused to join the Nation of Islam, as did Ali's parents. Brown respected Ali's choice to be a Muslim because it made Ali happy. Ali's mother was suspicious. She thought the only reason the Nation of Islam accepted her son was for his money and his popularity.

After the Liston fight, Ali traveled around the world. He spent a month traveling in the African countries of Ghana, Nigeria, and Egypt. He met many people in each country, including their leaders. Dressed in a white shirt and a narrow black tie, he waved to the crowds that came out to meet him.

When Ali returned to the United States, Herbert Muhammad introduced him to twenty-three-year-old Sonji Roi from Chicago, Illinois. Ali fell in love with her. She recalled that Ali asked her to marry him five minutes after they had met. In August 1964, just forty-one days after they had met, Muhammad Ali and Sonji Roi were married in Gary, Indiana. They had no time for a honeymoon. Ali had to return to Florida to train for his next fight.

Roi was an unusual choice for Ali. Muslim women were supposed to dress modestly, usually with clothing that covered them from head to foot. Roi worked in nightclubs and sometimes modeled for photographers. She wore makeup, smoked cigarettes, and refused to wear Muslim dress. Many of Ali's friends didn't like her.

Sonji and Ali in August 1964

Sonji tried to follow Islamic practices for a while. But she questioned the Nation of Islam. She didn't like the influence the group had over her husband's life. The marriage was shaky from the start.

Sonny, Howard, and Floyd

In May 1965, Ali was scheduled to meet Sonny Liston for a second fight, this time in Lewiston, Maine. The former champion had become the challenger. As soon as the fight began, Ali took the lead. Because he was so fast, he made Liston look even slower. Ali moved his upper body quickly, causing Liston to miss his punches.

Ali knocked out Liston in the first round with a short right punch. Some spectators didn't see the punch, but it hit Liston square on the temple. Liston crumbled and rolled over. He tried to get up, but he fell down again. Ali taunted him to get up. Liston staggered to his feet, but it was too late. The referee stopped the fight.

Ali yells at Liston to stand up and keep fighting in this 1965 fight.

Ali had proved again that he was heavyweight champion of the world. Even so, he said that he didn't feel different from anyone else. He promised that he'd never forget his people.

Ali was called the people's champion. He often took walks through poor neighborhoods and met fans. If he saw a homeless man, he might hand him a one-hundred-dollar bill or buy him a meal or a suit of clothes.

Ali didn't like to fly. So whenever possible, he and his staff went from fight to fight in a large bus. The words "Cassius Clay Enterprises" and "World's Most Colorful Fighter" were painted on the side of the bus. Wherever the bus stopped, people crowded around to meet Ali.

He rarely turned down an interview request. Even high school newspaper reporters were welcome to ask him questions. The ABC-TV sportscaster Howard Cosell was Ali's most famous interviewer. Cosell often pretended to be serious, while Ali told joke after joke. Fans loved their entertaining routine.

But Ali was not praised by everyone. Some reporters criticized Ali for using his fame to talk about his religious beliefs. Many people in the media and in the boxing community refused to use Ali's new name. They continued to call him Cassius Clay.

Some people thought Ali was too outspoken. They didn't like the way he insulted his opponents. And many people cheered against him. Other people thought that Ali's rhymes and remarks were just a way of making more publicity. Ali understood the show-business element of boxing. He didn't mind dominating the sports pages of newspapers.

Ali turned boxing into show business. Here he kids with performer Sammy Davis Jr.

Earlier Boxers: Johnson and Lewis

African American athletes had excelled in boxing long before Cassius Clay arrived on the scene. Young African American boxers like Clay owed a lot to two early African American heavyweight champions—Jack Johnson and Joe Louis *(below).*

Jack Johnson was born in 1878 in Galveston, Texas. He was known for his fast left and his excellent defense. In 1908, he fought for the heavyweight title, beating Tommy Burns in Sydney, Australia. Johnson's reign as the best boxer lasted seven years.

Joe Louis was popular through radio broadcasts of his fights. With excellent power in each hand, he was called unbeatable. He fought for the heavyweight title in 1937, knocking out James Braddock in the eighth round. Louis defended his title twenty-five times, losing only three bouts in his career. He held on to his heavyweight title from 1937 to 1949.

When Jack Johnson was champion, American society was strictly segregated. Most whites treated most blacks with hostility. African American fighters had a hard time proving their talents, because most white boxers refused to fight them. Johnson enraged many whites by showing that blacks could be superior athletes.

Joe Louis served in a segregated army unit during World War II (1939–1945). He never publicly questioned racial discrimination in the military or in American society. And because of his boxing success, he became a role model for African American youngsters from the 1950s onward.

"It's hard to be humble when you're as great as I am," he said.

In late 1965, Ali defended his title against Floyd Patterson, a former heavyweight champion, in Las Vegas, Nevada. Shy and quiet, Patterson had grown up in a tough section of Brooklyn, New York. In 1956, at the age of twenty-one, he had knocked out Archie Moore to become the heavyweight champion. But Patterson was now thirty. Ali was just twenty-three. Ali didn't like Patterson, who insisted on calling him Cassius Clay. Patterson thought the Nation of Islam was a danger to the United States.

Patterson and Ali fight in Las Vegas in 1965.

The crowd in Las Vegas included baseball star Joe DiMaggio, singer Frank Sinatra, and actor James Garner. From the very beginning of the fight, Ali didn't take Patterson seriously. He didn't throw a single punch in the first round. In the second round, Ali took control of the fight. It seemed as though he could knock out Patterson at any time. He dominated the bout, throwing jab after jab. He pounded Patterson so badly that the referee stopped the fight in the twelfth round. He gave Ali the win.

Ali successfully defended his title seven times through 1966 and 1967. He beat opponents George Chuvalo and Ernie Terrell by decision. He knocked out all the others–Zora Folley, Henry Cooper, Brian London, Karl Mildenberger, and Cleveland Williams. Ali seemed unbeatable.

CHAPTER 4 A DIFFERENT FIGHT

THE 1960S were a time of great change in the United States. In the mid-1960s, the United States began to support South Vietnam in a far-off war. This nation in Southeast Asia was fighting the Vietnam War (1954–1975) against the Communists of North Vietnam. At this time, the United States was strongly against Communism. The U.S. government had a long-standing policy of supporting any nation that fought against Communism. So the government sent hundreds of thousands of U.S. troops to South Vietnam to help fight the North Vietnamese. Many young American men had been killed by the North Vietnamese, also known as the Viet Cong.

(Above) **Ali often told people that he was "the prettiest fighter that ever lived."**

Many Americans, especially college students, opposed the war in Vietnam. Some young men refused to sign up for the draft (the process for placing men in the military). Every eighteen-year-old U.S. male was required to register, or sign up. When it was time to register, young men received a draft card in the mail. Some registrants returned their draft cards to the government or burned the cards in protest. More than ten thousand young men left the United States rather than serve in the U.S. military. Other men served four to five years in prison for evading, or refusing to be part of, the draft.

Ali and the Draft

Each man in the draft had a draft status, or class, which showed his fitness for being in the military. Muhammad Ali had a class of 1-Y. This meant he was considered unfit for military service except in an emergency. His devotion to boxing had taken him away from his studies in junior high and high school. He'd never studied much in school anyway. He scored poorly on army intelligence tests, particularly in the math section. "I have said I am the greatest," he reminded people, "Ain't nobody ever heard me say I am the smartest."

Draft Classes

During the Vietnam War, five basic classes of the draft existed. Within each class were specific definitions.

Class I-A:	a registrant who is available for military service
Class I-A-O:	a conscientious objector who is available only for military services that don't involve combat
Class I-C:	a member of the U.S. armed forces
Class I-D:	a member of the U.S. armed forces in reserve
Class I-S:	a registrant whose military service, by law, is deferred (put off) until he graduates from high school, reaches the age of twenty, or graduates from college
Class I-W:	a conscientious objector who, instead of joining the military, is working to maintain national health or safety
Class I-Y:	a registrant who is qualified for military service only in an emergency
Class II-A:	a deferment because the registrant is doing a job valued by the government
Class II-C:	a deferment because of doing a farming job
Class II-S:	a deferment because a registrant is a student
Class III-A:	a deferment for extreme hardship or because the registrant has a child
Class IV-A:	a registrant who has already served in the military and who is his family's only surviving son
Class IV-B:	a registrant who is a public official
Class IV-C:	a registrant who is not a U.S. citizen
Class IV-D:	a registrant who is a religious minister
Class IV-F:	a registrant who is not qualified for any military service
Class V-A:	a registrant who is over the age requirement for military service

Many people thought that Ali had done poorly on the tests to get out of the draft. They wanted to know how someone who wrote poetry and got so much media attention could be unfit for the military.

In February 1966, new laws lowered the intelligence requirements for army service. Ali was reclassified as 1-A. This meant that he could be drafted into the army.

At first, Ali didn't pay much attention to Vietnam. But as more people began talking about his draft status, he began to speak out against the war. He believed that African Americans had a more pressing battle–the battle for equal rights–to fight at home. "I don't have nothing against them Viet Cong," he told reporters. "If I have to die I'll die fighting for freedom here." He also recited a rhyme:

IT'S A FACT!

U.S. soldiers called North Vietnamese soldiers the Viet Cong. This name was a mixture of Vietnamese words that meant "Vietnamese Communist."

Keep asking me, no matter how long
On the war in Vietnam, I sing this song
I ain't got no quarrel with the Viet Cong.

Ali, here attending a Nation of Islam convention in Chicago, Illinois, asked not to be put in the army for religious reasons.

Ali claimed that his religious beliefs prevented him from serving in the military. The Nation of Islam preached peace, he explained. The group also considered itself a separate nation and refused to take part in a war for the United States. Ali applied to become a conscientious objector, a person who legally doesn't serve in the military for moral and religious reasons. Officials denied Ali's request.

THE CALL UP

Ali was called to join the U.S. Army in April 1967. The army offered to put him in the Special Services, the unit that entertained the troops. He could visit with troops and box in exhibition matches instead of fighting in combat.

Many people in the boxing community encouraged Ali to take the army's offer. They didn't want him to risk his career and his popularity by saying no to the U.S. Army. The penalty for avoiding the draft was usually five years in prison and a five thousand dollar fine. (The court could charge higher fines.)

Ali arrived at the U.S. Armed Forces Examining and Entrance Station in Houston, Texas, on the morning of April 28, 1967. He was one of twenty-six draftees called to the station that day. Crowds of antiwar demonstrators chanted outside the building on Ali's behalf. Reporters waited to find out whether or not he would become a soldier.

Inside, Ali and the other young men filled out forms and took physical exams. At about 1:00 P.M., they reported to a ceremony room, where an officer read the draftees' names. When a man heard his name, he was supposed to step forward. By stepping

Ali reports to the U.S. Army center in Houston, Texas in 1967.

forward, he had officially become part of the U.S. military. Each man stepped forward as his name was called. Then it was Ali's turn.

The officer called out Cassius Marcellus Clay, but Ali didn't move. He called Ali's original name again. Ali looked straight ahead. This time, he was led from the room. A lieutenant formally told Ali of the punishment for draft evasion. He would be given one last chance to step forward when his name was called.

The officer said his name a third time. Ali still didn't move. In a written statement afterward, he explained that, as a Muslim minister, he believed that he shouldn't have to go into military service. Again his request was denied.

Outside the building, the station's commanding officer told the media that Ali had refused to join the army. The news spread immediately. Ali would go to court for draft evasion. In a four-page statement prepared ahead of time, Ali explained: "I find I cannot be true to my belief in my religion in accepting such a call."

The Court Battle

Parents of young men serving in Vietnam called Ali a traitor to the United States. Former heavyweight champion Joe Louis, who had enlisted in the army during World War II, commented, "I think he should fight for his country." Kentucky lawmakers condemned Ali, saying that "his attitude brings discredit to all loyal Kentuckians and to the names of thousands who gave their lives for this country during his lifetime."

Others were more supportive. "No matter what you think of Muhammad Ali's religion," preached civil rights leader Martin Luther King Jr., "you certainly have to admire his courage." A group of famous African American athletes called Ali to a meeting in Cleveland. Football star Jim Brown, basketball greats Bill Russell and Lew Alcindor (later known as Kareem Abdul-Jabbar), and others talked with Ali about his position against the war. After the meeting, the athletes announced their support for his decision.

The World Boxing Association and the New York State Athletic Commission stripped him of the heavyweight title and took away his boxing license. In an unusual move, the commission didn't hold a public hearing to discuss the decision. "We can take away a fighter's title for any acts which we consider not [right for] the best interests of boxing," explained Edwin B. Dooley, the chairman of the New York State Athletic Commission. Every other state's athletic commission followed New York's

It's a Fact!

Baseball legend Jackie Robinson, the first African American to play major league baseball, thought Ali should join the army. He said, "I think he's hurting the morale of a lot of young [African American] soldiers over in Vietnam and the tragedy to me is that Cassius has made millions of dollars off the American public. Now he's not willing to show his appreciation to a country that's giving him a fantastic opportunity."

lead. "It was an outrage, an absolute disgrace," said Howard Cosell about the decision to take away Ali's license without a hearing.

Ali's court trial began on June 19, 1967. Mobs of people showed up in the courtroom to support him. Dressed in a dark suit and tie, Ali solemnly defended his position. He didn't burn his draft card as others had, he told the court. Instead, he was fighting the draft legally. Ali was not afraid to go to jail if he lost.

The judge found Ali guilty of draft evasion and gave him the maximum sentence–a fine of ten thousand dollars and five years in jail. Ali's lawyers immediately appealed. This is a legal way to ask the court to review its decision. The appeal was successful, and Ali didn't have to go to jail. But his license was still taken away, so he couldn't earn a living by boxing. His passport was canceled, so he wasn't able to travel overseas for boxing matches.

Speaking Out

People still wanted to see Ali. But instead of watching him fight, they heard him speak. He traveled around the country. He defended his position on the draft and explained the philosophy

Ali addresses a Nation of Islam meeting in Houston, Texas, in 1967.

of the Nation of Islam. He talked about his fights. He spoke at major colleges and universities. Hundreds of students gathered on steps and leaned out of windows to listen to him.

Ali always started his speeches by saying that he was still the heavyweight champion of the world. "Everybody knows I'm the champion," he said. "My ghost will haunt all the arenas. I'll be there, wearing a sheet and whispering 'Ali-e-e-e! Ali-e-e-e!'"

Ali had lost his title and his career. But he cared more about his personal beliefs than about his fame or fortune. "The wealth of America and the friendship of all the people who support the war would be nothing if I'm not content [inside] and if I'm not in accord with the will of Almighty Allah."

CHAPTER 5

PEOPLE'S CHAMPION

ALI TRAVELED in his bus to speak to college students about his beliefs. When he didn't have a speaking job, he appeared on game shows and talk shows. "I will die before I sell out my people for... money," he said on one TV show. At the age of twenty-four, he had left behind his title, the million-dollar prize money, and all the extras given to the heavyweight champion. He told reporters that he had sacrificed nearly $9 million in advertisements, film deals, and record contracts for his beliefs.

He still made money from his fame–although far less than he would have made as a fighter. He received $200,000 for his autobiography, *The Greatest: My Own Story.* He endorsed, or helped sell, products. He opened a chain of fast-food restaurants called Champburgers, which quickly went out of business. He worked with a group of filmmakers on *A/K/A Cassius Clay,* a documentary about his career.

It's a Fact!

While away from boxing, Ali appeared in the title role of a New York musical called *Buck White.* He was almost unrecognizable in a large black wig, a mustache, and a beard. Not a bad singer, he drew good reviews.

Ali and Belinda

By this time, Ali and Sonji Roi had divorced. She hadn't followed traditional Muslim practices, he charged in the divorce papers. Sonji blamed the Nation of Islam for the failed marriage. "They wanted to control his entire life," she said. "I wasn't going to take on all the Muslims." The marriage ended bitterly.

Ali began to date other women. Many women were interested in the handsome fighter. But he preferred to be with a woman who shared his faith. Seventeen-year-old Belinda Boyd had been raised as a Black Muslim. She was soft-spoken and followed Islamic customs. She had first met Muhammad in 1961 at a Black Muslim school in Chicago, where he was the visiting Olympic champion. The couple met again a few years later at a Nation of Islam convention and soon began to date.

"'You're gonna be my wife,'" she said he told her. "He didn't ask me, he told me." On August 17,

Ali and Belinda on their wedding day

1967, Muhammad and Belinda were married in Chicago. She joined him on his speaking tour of college campuses. Ten months later, their first daughter, Maryum Ali, was born.

Coming Back

In 1968, the World Boxing Association organized an eight-man tournament to replace Ali as world champion. In the last round of the tournament, Jimmy Ellis fought Jerry Quarry for the heavyweight title. Ellis won by a close decision.

Meanwhile, Howard Cosell and a few other journalists and politicians helped Ali get back his boxing license. In September 1970, a New York court ruled that the recall of Ali's license had been unreasonable. State senator Leroy Johnson of Georgia helped arrange a bout for Ali in Atlanta, Georgia.

The fight was scheduled for October 1970 against Jerry Quarry, a strong puncher. Some people felt that Ali shouldn't be allowed to fight. Both fighters received death threats. Ali received a package with a dead black dog and a note that read: "We know how to handle black draft-dodging dogs in Georgia. Stay out of Atlanta."

Ali training in early 1970

But the fight was on. The crowd was filled with celebrities, including actors Bill Cosby and Sidney Poitier, civil rights leader Jesse Jackson, and Martin Luther King Jr.'s widow, Coretta Scott King. Limousines double-parked outside the arena. Women wore furs and pearls, and men dressed in tuxedos.

Three and a half years after he'd been expelled from boxing, Ali returned to the ring. He was twenty-eight years old, and the best years of his career were gone. He could no longer dance for fifteen rounds. His movements were not as graceful, and he had lost some of his quickness. But he was talented enough to find a different way to fight.

He came out throwing punches and opened up a large cut over Quarry's eye in the third round. The referee stopped the fight. Annoyed, Quarry didn't want to stop fighting. But Ali had his first victory since the draft.

The crowd went wild. Ali was back. Two months later, he fought tough Oscar Bonavena in Madison Square Garden. He knocked him down three times in the fifteenth round before finally knocking him out.

Fighting Frazier

Ali's next fight would be against Joe Frazier, the world champion. Frazier had turned pro in 1965. He had had twenty-three knockouts in twenty-six fights and was undefeated.

Ali weighed 215 pounds. Frazier weighed less, at 205 pounds. Standing five feet eleven inches, Frazier was four inches shorter and two years younger than Ali. Frazier was a powerful fighter, who hit his opponents quickly, over and over. His best weapon was his left hook, and he had a powerful right. He chose effectiveness over style.

In contrast, Ali was a smooth stylist who could outpunch his opponents. His blows seemed to come from everywhere. He held his hands low and moved quickly. He leaned away from punches instead of stepping away from them.

The two fighters were opposites in personality too. Ali loved talking to reporters and being the center of attention. He called Frazier dumb and a gorilla. "Joe has always been a little slow in making out whether or not I'm serious or putting him on," Ali said. "He's not sure whether he is in on the joke or the joke is on him." Ali picked on Frazier's South Carolina accent, his grammar, vocabulary, and intelligence. "Joe Frazier is too ugly to be champ. Joe Frazier is too dumb to be champ," he said. "Everybody who's black wants me to keep winning." He shouted into the microphones, "I am the greatest!"

Frazier, quiet and brooding, was businesslike and focused on the fight, not on the show. He fought for the sport of it and to earn money to support his wife and children. "This is just another man, another fight, another payday," he

Frazier and Ali trade insults in late 1970 as members of the press look on.

said beforehand. Frazier acknowledged that it would not be an easy fight. Both men were good fighters. Angered by Ali's insults, he insisted on calling him Cassius Clay. "If I pass him in the desert and he's thirsting," Frazier warned, "I'll drive right by."

The fight was set for March 8, 1971, at Madison Square Garden in New York City. Each fighter would earn $2.5 million. But only one would be the heavyweight champion of the world. Ali was an 8–5 favorite among people who bet on fights. A month before the fight, all the tickets had been sold. On the night of the fight, blocks and blocks of streets around Madison Square Garden were closed off. The crowd included celebrities, such as Diana Ross and Frank Sinatra.

After the fight started, Ali played to the crowd. He talked to Frazier and didn't take the first five rounds seriously. To many people in the crowd, he looked like the Ali of old times–moving, shuffling, ducking, and throwing sharp punches. Frazier was determined to win. He threw hard punches with both hands to Ali's body, trying to weaken him. Frazier's punches landed everywhere. Ali wasn't as fast as he had once been. His legs were slower, and he was slower to move out of the way. He absorbed more tough punches than he had in any previous fight. His body became red with Frazier's beating.

Frazier was taking a beating too. His lip started bleeding, and his face swelled up. In the eleventh round, Frazier threw a left hook that wobbled the tired Ali, hurting him more than he'd ever been hurt in his career.

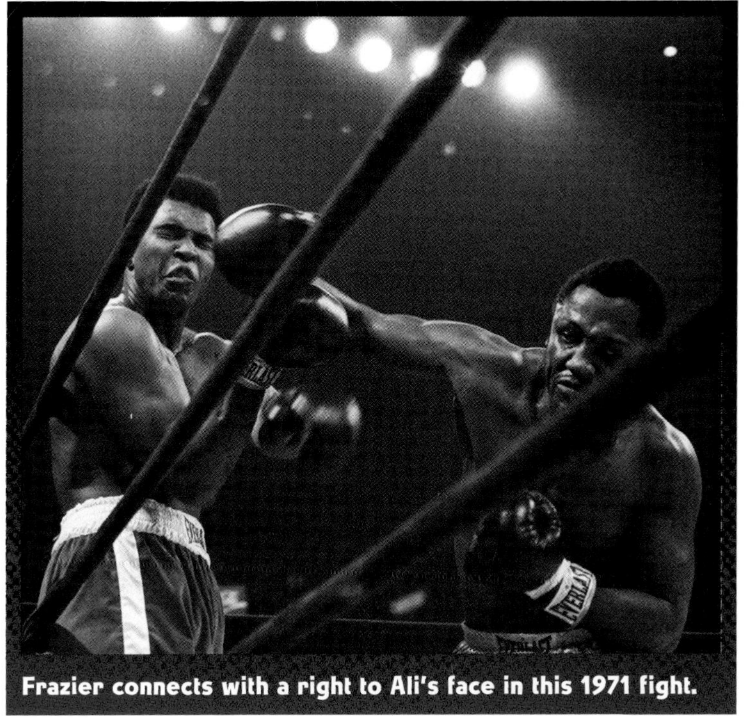
Frazier connects with a right to Ali's face in this 1971 fight.

The next four rounds were just as brutal. In the fifteenth and final round, Frazier called on everything he had. He threw a massive left hook that landed on the tip of Ali's chin. Ali fell on his back with his feet up in the air. He rolled over on his side and then got up at the count of six. (Boxers have until the count of eight.)

Frazier won the fight by a unanimous decision. Both fighters were exhausted. Both of

It's a Fact!

After being knocked down, a boxer has until the referee counts to eight to get back up. This is called a standing eight-count. During this time, the opponent must stand in a neutral corner. If a boxer takes three standing-eights in a round or four in a bout, the referee stops the fight. The opponent is then declared the winner.

their faces were bruised, swollen, and misshapen. Both were taken to the hospital after the fight. It was Ali's first loss.

Ali said afterward, "What hurt most wasn't the money that losing cost me. It wasn't the punches I took. It was knowing that my title was gone."

By this time, Ali's draft case had reached the U.S. Supreme Court. In June 1971, the court reversed Ali's conviction. The judges ruled that Ali was a conscientious objector. All criminal charges against him were dropped.

CHAPTER 6

The Comeback

With his legal struggles finally behind him, Ali began his comeback in the ring. During the rest of 1971, he beat Jimmy Ellis in Houston, Texas, in Ali's thirty-second fight. He won a decision over Buster Mathis and knocked out a West German fighter named Jurgen Blin in the seventh round.

He met three former opponents the following year. George Chuvalo lost again, just as he had six years earlier. Jerry Quarry thought he had a chance to beat Ali, but he lost in the seventh round. Thirty-seven-year-old Floyd Patterson met Ali for a second time and also lasted to the seventh round. In Ali's last fight of 1972, he knocked out former light heavyweight champion Bob Foster, who weighed forty-one pounds less than Ali, in the eighth round.

Deer Lake

In 1972, Ali opened a training camp at Deer Lake, Pennsylvania. He built a gym, a dining hall, and cabins for sparring (practice) partners and guests. He hired his own cook and a large staff. Ali and his team ate at one large, round table. Water came from a well.

It's a Fact!

Boulders on the Deer Lake property were marked with the names of fighters. The centerpiece was a forty-ton boulder representing Joe Louis.

Ali was rarely alone at Deer Lake. As many as fifty people surrounded him. The people included his friend Bundini Brown; his trainer, Angelo Dundee; his manager, Herbert Muhammad; and his brother Rudy, now named Rahaman. Photographer Howard Bingham took thousands of pictures of the champ.

The door at Deer Lake was always open. Fans, reporters, and the public were welcome. At first, the Deer Lake neighbors were suspicious of Ali's camp. But they soon learned they were just as welcome as anyone. People came from miles around to watch Ali train. He signed autographs and posed for pictures. In the evening, he did magic tricks to entertain the visitors.

When he wasn't training or traveling, Ali lived in a sixteen-room mansion in Chicago with Belinda and their children. In addition to Maryum, Muhammad and Belinda had twin girls named Rasheeda and Jamillah and a boy, Muhammad Jr. Sometimes the whole family stayed at Deer Lake.

Ali and his daughters Maryum *(front)*, Jamillah, and Rasheeda *(behind her father)* stroll by the Deer Lake monument to Sonny Liston.

Belinda Ali

"Muhammad absolutely loved the children," Belinda recalled, "but he didn't have the patience to spend full-time with them." He was usually away from home, training or fighting. Maryum Ali didn't like to watch her father's fights. She was afraid he would get hurt. Even when Ali was at home with the family, Maryum remembers, reporters, staff, and visitors were constantly streaming in and out of the house. "There weren't enough of those times when we were a family unit," she says.

More Fights

In February 1973, Ali won a decision over Joe Bugner, his tenth win in a row since the fight with Frazier. He came into the ring wearing a long robe decorated with jewels, a gift from his rock-and-roll friend Elvis Presley. The words "People's Champion" were on the back.

One month later, he faced Ken Norton in San Diego, California. Norton, a former U.S. Marine and a former sparring partner of Joe Frazier's, wasn't considered much of an opponent. But he was well trained and had a decent jab.

Norton's coach was Frazier's trainer, Eddie Futch. Futch instructed his fighter to aim for Ali's body. Instead, Norton ended up breaking Ali's jaw in the second round. Ali didn't want the fight stopped. He fought the full twelve rounds and lost by a split decision–a 2-1 vote of the judges. Spectators called out, "That loudmouth is finished!" Ali received a note that read, "The butterfly has lost its wings, the bee has lost its sting."

It took six months for his jaw to heal, and then he faced Norton again. This time, Ali trained harder and took Norton more seriously. The effort paid off. He won the fight by a unanimous decision. He fought once more that year, winning a decision over Rudi Lubbers in Jakarta, Indonesia, in October.

More than anything, Ali wanted a rematch with Joe Frazier. Frazier had fought only twice that year. He had lost the heavyweight title to young George Foreman in Kingston, Jamaica, in January 1973. Foreman had knocked down Frazier six times in two rounds before the referee stopped the fight.

In January 1974, Ali and Frazier finally met again, though not for a world title fight. The two fighters faced each other in Madison Square Garden. The promoter, who set up the fight, guaranteed each man $850,000. The Garden was sold out, and Ali was a slight favorite.

The fight was very different from the first time the two boxers had met. Ali was in much better condition than before. He moved quickly around the ring. He weakened most of Frazier's power and punches by holding on to him. Both fighters threw far fewer punches than they had before. At the end of the twelfth round, Ali was the winner by a unanimous decision.

Frazier asked for a rematch. But first, Ali wanted the heavyweight title back. He needed to fight twenty-six-year-old George Foreman to get it.

Fighting George

The "Rumble in the Jungle" would take place in Africa. Ali and Foreman would fight in Kinshasa, Zaire (modern Congo), that October. The bout, organized by the government of Zaire and boxing promoter Don King, was originally scheduled for September 25. But Foreman cut his eye while sparring, and this put off the match until October 30. Each fighter would receive $5 million.

Don King

Born in 1931, Don King became the first major African American boxing promoter in 1974, when he set up Ali's fight against George Foreman in Zaire. He went on to promote more than five hundred world championship fights.

His boxing promotions drew large crowds and earned huge amounts. He made himself and the fighters he represented rich. But many fighters later accused King of cheating them out of money. Meanwhile, King has gone to court numerous times to defend accusations of fraud and of not paying taxes. He remains a famous figure in the boxing world.

Foreman–like his hero, Sonny Liston–was considered unbeatable. Born in Marshall, Texas, Foreman had a record forty wins, thirty-seven knockouts, and no losses. As a young man, he'd been a neighborhood troublemaker until he'd turned to boxing. He'd won the Olympic heavyweight gold medal in 1968 in Mexico City, Mexico. He was a tremendous puncher with both hands.

In Zaire, Foreman kept to himself. "I am the most boring man in the world," he said at a press conference. Ali, on the other hand, promoted himself and the fight. He gave interviews, went to press conferences, and signed autographs. "It's a great feeling being in a country operated by black people," Ali told reporters. The crowds were overwhelmingly in favor of Ali. People lined the streets, eager to see him and join him in his morning runs.

The fight started at 3:00 A.M., so it could be broadcast live back in the United States. In the early rounds, the powerful Foreman went after Ali in the ring and pinned him against the ropes. Ali used his "rope-a-dope" technique. He covered his head, rested against the ropes, and let Foreman hit him in the body. This technique tends to wear out

Ali and Foreman spar during the "Rumble in the Jungle" in 1974.

the hitter. Ali taunted Foreman. He called him big George. He also taunted Foreman about his strength.

The crowd was surprised that Ali could hold up to so much power. But Foreman became tired in the seventh round. In the eighth, Ali threw a hard left and then a right. Foreman had run out of gas. Ali knocked him down with punch after punch.

Ali said Foreman's punches hurt the most in the first round. But as the fight went on, they came in slower and didn't hurt as much. Declared the winner, Ali raised his hands in his famous pose of victory. Angelo Dundee and Bundini Brown jumped for joy. Fans climbed into the ring to hug Ali, who had finally regained his title.

He was named Fighter of the Year by boxing's top magazine, *Ring,* and Sportsman of the Year by *Sports Illustrated* magazine. Once considered a traitor to his country, Ali received an invitation to the White House to visit with U.S. president Gerald Ford.

The Thrilla in Manila

Ali defended his title successfully three more times in 1975. He stopped Chuck Wepner in the fifteenth round and Ron Lyle in the eleventh. He won a unanimous decision over Joe Bugner.

Next was the rematch with Joe Frazier in Manila, the Philippines. The bout was also known as the "Thrilla in Manila." Ali recited a rhyme he'd created.

It will be a killer
And a chiller
And a thrilla
When I get the gorilla
In Manila

During training, Ali punched a large stuffed gorilla at his Deer Lake training camp. "Joe Frazier, Joe Frazier," he repeated with each punch in front of a large crowd and television cameras. At a press conference before the fight, Ali leaned across the table at his opponent. He pretended to hit Frazier, who looked back in amusement. Ali promised Frazier that he would hit him most on the head. He playfully hit a black plastic gorilla and shouted that he had to capture the gorilla to the crowd. But Frazier was out for revenge. "I'm going to make him quit. No matter what name he goes by, he's gonna quit," Frazier insisted.

It's a Fact!

Joe Frazier's eldest son, fourteen-year-old Marvis, went to Manila to watch the bout. After the fight, Marvis was upset. Ali asked to see him. He tried to calm Marvis by saying, "Tell your father all the stuff I said about him—I didn't mean it. Your father's a [great] man. I couldn't have taken the punches he took tonight.

In the Philippines, billboards advertised the "Fight of a Lifetime." Ali was the center of attention.

This wasn't only because of his religious beliefs. His personal life was also bringing him publicity. Muhammad and Belinda Ali had been married for eight years. But Ali brought another woman, Veronica Porche, to the fight. Ferdinand Marcos, president of the Philippines, assumed that Porche was Ali's wife. Ali didn't correct the president's mistake.

Reporters pounced on the story. Ali shrugged off their criticism. He had met Veronica while preparing for the Foreman fight. She had won a beauty contest to become one of four poster girls hired to promote the event. Ali had fallen in love with her. By this time, Ali had fathered two more daughters, Miyah and Khaliah, born to women other than his wife.

When the news about Veronica Porche became public, Belinda Ali flew from Chicago to Manila. With the press tagging behind her, she went to her husband's hotel room. A noisy argument followed. Then Belinda turned right around and flew back home to Chicago. She and Ali were close to divorce.

Despite the ups and downs in his personal life, Ali focused on the fight. More than seven hundred million viewers would watch the fight on television. Ali would earn $6 million and Frazier would earn $3 million, no matter who won or lost. Ali was favored to win.

President Marcos and his wife, Imelda, were seated ringside. "Smokin' Joe" was written on the back of Frazier's robe. When the announcer introduced Ali, he raised his hands and walked around the ring as the crowd shouted his name. The fighters talked to each other from the opening bell. Both men came out punching.

IT'S A FACT!

The nickname Smokin' Joe referred to Frazier's quick, powerful punches.

Frazier had Ali on the ropes in the third round. Ali's hands went up to protect his face and head. Then he suddenly whipped his hands out and started punching Frazier's head. The fight went back and forth. Frazier took charge and then retreated. Then Ali did the same. Ali dominated in the beginning, Frazier in the middle, and Ali at the end. They both looked exhausted.

Ali could barely come out in the thirteenth round. He tried to knock out Frazier, throwing

Frazier begins to crumble in the 1975 fight in Manila.

nonstop punches to Frazier's face and body. Frazier, wobbly, refused to go down. They both walked slowly to their corners. Frazier was bleeding badly from inside his mouth. His left eye was completely closed. He had difficulty seeing out of his right eye, and he was spitting up blood. They slugged it out for another round.

Before the bell rang for the fifteenth round, Frazier's trainer, Eddie Futch, asked his fighter how he felt. Frazier said that he couldn't see Ali's right, only his left. "Sit down, son. It's all over," Futch said. "But no one will ever forget what you did here today." Not wanting to see his fighter permanently injured, Futch threw in the towel to show that Frazier was done. Ali had to be helped out of the ring to his dressing room. He said that the end of the fight "was like death. Closest thing to dyin' that I know of." Badly battered, he was still the winner.

CHAPTER 7

CALLING IT QUITS

(Above) By the time Ali was in his mid-thirties, he was considered too old for boxing.

IN 1976, Ali turned thirty-four years old. In the boxing world, he was old. As a fighter gets older, his legs move more slowly. He can see a punch coming, but he can't move out of its way as quickly. He knows all the techniques, but his legs and punches no longer have as much snap. When they age, some boxers retire. They feel they can't keep up with the younger crowd and are fearful of being injured. Others, like Ali, continue to fight.

Final Fights

Ali defended his title four times that year. He knocked out Jean Pierre Coopman and beat Jimmy Young by decision. He stopped Richard Dunn and met Ken Norton for a third time. In this fifteen-round decision in favor of Ali, Ali was slower and didn't punch as hard. He spent more time moving around than throwing punches. When the decision was announced, Norton held his head in his hands. "It was just crushing to me," he said.

Muhammad and Belinda Ali divorced in September 1976. Their four children remained with their mother in Chicago. Muhammad moved in with Veronica Porche, and they had a daughter, Hana. When the baby was ten months old, Ali and Veronica got married in Los Angeles, California.

Ali defended his title twice in 1977, winning fifteen-round decisions over both Alfredo Evangelista and Ernie Shavers. Shavers was one of the hardest-hitting punchers in the heavyweight division. Ali absorbed more punches than he had in the past. But he was still good enough to beat these opponents.

Ali vs. Spinks

His next opponent was twenty-four-year-old Leon Spinks. The fight was scheduled for February 1978. Spinks was not expected to give Ali any trouble, mostly because of Spinks's poor training habits. Spinks and his older brother, Michael, had both won medals at the 1976 Olympics in Montreal, Canada. The idea of beating another Olympic medalist interested Ali. He had beaten gold medalists Patterson, Frazier, and Foreman.

Born in East Saint Louis, Illinois, Leon Spinks was a former U.S. Marine and a respected amateur fighter. After the Olympics, Spinks turned pro. Before he fought Ali, his record was six wins, no losses, with one draw against Scott LeDoux.

Even though Ali hadn't fought in five months, he didn't take Spinks seriously. At the age of thirty-six, Ali weighed 242 pounds. He had worked out less and had sparred for only twenty rounds. Spinks was in shape and ready.

Ali didn't fight hard for the first six rounds. He expected his young opponent to get tired. But it never happened. Although Spinks was a wild puncher, Ali was not in good enough shape to move out of the

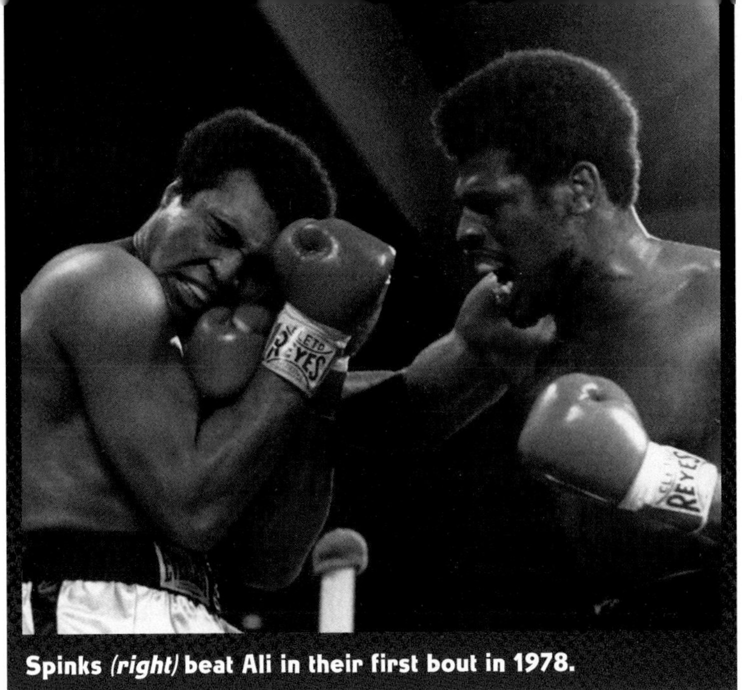
Spinks *(right)* beat Ali in their first bout in 1978.

way. His own punches had very little power. Spinks remained fresh throughout the fight and stunned the boxing world by winning a fifteen-round split decision. It was Spinks's night of triumph.

"I just couldn't leave boxing that way, losing an embarrassing fight like that," Ali said afterward. He said that Spinks had only borrowed his title. Ali demanded a rematch.

Ali trained hard for his world heavyweight championship rematch with Spinks. The bout

IT'S A FACT!

In a split decision, two of three judges agree on the winner. Sometimes the three judges will call the bout a draw. In a draw, no winner is named.

was to be held in September 1978 in New Orleans, Louisiana. Ali pushed himself in training, running three to five miles before breakfast every day and sparring for more than two hundred rounds.

In front of more than sixty thousand people in the New Orleans Superdome, Ali was in command from the opening round. He jabbed Spinks all night long, never letting him become aggressive. Spinks lacked the fire that he had had in the first fight. His punches kept missing. Ali recaptured his title by a unanimous decision.

Spinks said afterward that Ali had always been his idol and that he still was. Ali became the first man in boxing history to win the world heavyweight championship three times.

First Retirement

Finally, in 1979, Muhammad Ali announced his retirement. After nineteen years and fifty-nine professional bouts, it was time to call it quits. By that time, he and Veronica had had a second daughter, Laila. The family lived in Los Angeles.

Ali kept busy in many ways. He went on a speaking tour. He helped sell Idaho potatoes and

Ali relaxes with daughters Laila *(left)* and Hana.

other products. He acted in a four-hour television miniseries called *Freedom Road.* Ali played an ex-slave and Civil War veteran who eventually becomes a U.S. senator. He traveled to Bangladesh in South Asia and rode in a motorcade through crowded streets. Citizens paid their respects by singing songs. He rode elephants and playfully sparred with children.

U.S. president Jimmy Carter then asked Ali to go to Africa. He wanted the champ to drum up support for the U.S. boycott of (decision to stay away from) the 1980 Olympics. The Games were scheduled to be held in Moscow, then the capital of the Soviet Union. President Carter strongly opposed the Soviet Union's recent invasion of the country of Afghanistan. By not going to the Games, the president was showing America's disapproval of the invasion.

Ali visited with African leaders in Tanzania, Kenya, Nigeria, Liberia, and Senegal. He explained the U.S. position on the boycott. The trip was not very successful, because many African nations got money from the Soviet Union. But as usual, Ali was a hit.

Return to the Ring

Retirement didn't last very long. After Ali stepped down, Larry Holmes became the heavyweight champion by beating Ken Norton in a fifteen-round decision. Ali thought he could beat Holmes easily. He knew Holmes and his style of boxing. The two fighters had sparred with each other at Deer Lake. Holmes felt that he had to beat Ali to gain the respect of the boxing community.

So two years after his last fight, the thirty-eight-year-old champion came out of retirement. "He's only Larry Holmes, and he's nothin'," said Ali. "Holmes must go. I'll eat him up.

"If Ali stays in front of me, he's gonna get knocked out early," returned Holmes. "Now he's gonna find out how it feels to be an old man fighting a good fast young man." Holmes predicted that he'd defeat Ali. He thought Ali was too old and that this bout was Holmes's to win.

Most people on Ali's staff thought that he shouldn't fight Holmes. Ali was beginning to have health problems. He sometimes slurred his speech and didn't always seem alert. He occasionally fell asleep during interviews. People wondered if Ali's brain had been affected by blows to the head–a problem common to boxers. Medical tests showed that Ali was in poor health. But the Nevada State Athletic Commission allowed the fight to be held in Las Vegas in October 1980.

Ali weighed in at 217, Holmes at 211. For the first few rounds, Ali looked fantastic. He had lost 43 pounds, and he moved quickly. But his punches weren't strong. Holmes was respectful of Ali for the

Larry Holmes *(right)* erased any hopes of another comeback for Ali.

first five rounds. He didn't attack as hard as he could have. And then the fight became painful to watch. Ali was not the same fighter who had overwhelmed Liston, Patterson, Foreman, and Frazier. Ali's punches were weak, while Holmes performed at his best.

The judges awarded every round to Holmes. As the winner was announced, Holmes had tears in his eyes. He had beaten the Greatest, who didn't look that great anymore. At the press conference after the fight, Ali told Holmes that he had won clean and fair. He then advised the crowd to support Holmes until Ali returned as champ.

It's a Fact!

Ali often wore a boxing robe that carried the letters *GOAT*. These stood for Greatest of All Time.

The Last Bout

A little more than a year later, Ali decided to fight again to test the skills he had left. Trainer Angleo Dundee wanted Ali to stop fighting. He thought Ali had nothing to prove. But Ali disagreed. He knew he should stop fighting, but he felt he needed to try one more time.

Trevor Berbick was considered an easy opponent. He'd lost a fifteen-round decision to Larry Holmes eight months earlier. "I'm gonna mess 'em all up by [beating] Berbick and then becoming the first forty-year-old man to ever win the heavyweight title. Get ready for the shocker,"

It's a Fact!

During his professional career, Ali was never knocked out. He retired after sixty-one bouts with a record of fifty-six wins, thirty-seven knockouts, and just five losses. He was the first man to win the heavyweight title three times. (Evander Holyfield equaled this record and later won a fourth title.)

Ali warned. "I'm gonna mess up the world."

The matchup with Berbick was held in Nassau, in the Bahamas, on December 11, 1981. Ali weighed 236 pounds–more than when he had fought Holmes. Berbick, an awkward fighter who was difficult to hit, was not much of a puncher. But he was the aggressor and won by a decision. This fight would be Ali's last. It was a sad ending to a brilliant career. "Father Time caught up with me," Ali announced. "I'm finished."

CHAPTER 8
"I AIN'T DEAD YET!"

AFTER ALI QUIT BOXING for good, he traveled around the world. He made personal appearances and spread the word of the Nation of Islam. He helped sell products and promoted boxing matches for a year or two.

***(Above)* Even after retiring, Ali was still popular with fans.**

But his health continued to get worse. Doctors diagnosed his condition as Parkinson's syndrome, an illness of the brain. He began to move and speak very slowly. His hands trembled, and his face often looked blank.

Parkinson's Syndrome

Ali suffers from Parkinson's syndrome, one of the forms of a broader brain disease called parkinsonism. No known cure exists for the disease, which affects a person's ability to move and speak. Medicines can help control symptoms. These include the slight shaking of the arms, jaw, legs, or face; slowness of movement; and shaky balance. Most doctors agree that a past history of trauma to the head—as in multiple blows during a long career in boxing—may be a cause of Parkinson's syndrome.

Many doctors believed that Ali's condition was caused by repeated blows to the head from boxing.

Ali's fortune had also gone down. He had earned tens of millions of dollars in the ring. He had donated hundreds of thousands of dollars to charities, to people in need, and to the Nation of Islam. Millions more had been lost on bad investments. Many of his business ideas had failed.

Personal Changes

His marriage to Veronica Porche also failed. In 1986, the couple divorced. Ali quickly remarried, this time to Lonnie Williams, a Muslim woman who had grown up on his street in Louisville. She was just a little girl when Olympic champion

Cassius Clay had visited his hometown and played with the kids in the neighborhood.

Every time he went to Louisville, Ali continued to visit Williams and her family. Even as she grew up and went off to college, she and Ali stayed in touch. After graduating from college, Lonnie moved to Los Angeles and converted to Islam.

"What happened was, our friendship had become very strong," she said, "which is the way I think all marriages should start." On November 19, 1986, the couple was married. Ali and Lonnie adopted a son, Asaad, a few years later.

Altogether, Ali has nine children. He hasn't spent as much time with his children as other fathers have. During his career, he was usually training, fighting, or traveling.

Ali and Lonnie in 2004

For the children, life with a famous father wasn't always easy. Everyone knew about Ali's divorces and love affairs. When he divorced Belinda and later Veronica, he was also separated from his children with them. His daughters born outside of marriage spent even less time with their father.

Most of Ali's children are grown and live in different cities around the United States. "I didn't have as much time as I wanted to teach them. . . . I wasn't really around to raise them," Ali says. But his daughter Laila has followed in his footsteps and has her own career in boxing.

Ali's finances are in better shape, and his health is fair. "People say I talk so slow today. That's no surprise," he says. "I calculate I've taken 29,000 punches, but I earned [millions of dollars] and I saved half of it. I may talk slow, but my mind is okay."

A Quieter Life

Ali, Lonnie, and Asaad live a comfortable life. They have a home in Los Angeles and a small farm in Michigan. Ali allows the Deer Lake training camp to be used as a home for single mothers. The camp still holds the boulders painted with the names of great fighters.

Laila Ali

"Right now, people don't know me," Laila Ali *(below)* told *People* magazine in 1999. "They say, 'We'll see what she can do.' Well, I can't wait to get in the ring and show them." From the first bell, Laila seemed to have her father's talent as well as his self-confidence. At the age of twenty-one, she won her first professional boxing match, with a knockout just thirty-one seconds into the first round. She went on to win three more fights by knockout. This impressive beginning made her father proud. "You're good," her father told her as she sparred with him during the 1999 *People* interview. "I don't have to give you any pointers."

Laila has since fought and beaten Jackie Frazier-Lyde, the daughter of Joe Frazier. Laila first won the Super Middleweight champion title in 2002 and successfully defended it in 2004.

More than twenty years after he left the boxing ring, Ali continues to make appearances. Crowds still gather for autographs from the Greatest. He personally answers the hundreds of fan letters that he receives each month. He welcomes fans, neighbors, and friends to his home. He never turns down a request for an autograph.

In the 1990s, Ali served as an unofficial ambassador for the United States. He traveled to Iraq in 1990 to meet with Iraqi leader Saddam Hussein. Hussein, a fellow Muslim, was holding three hundred Americans as prisoners. Ali hoped to gain their freedom. He was partially successful. He returned to the United States ten days later with fifteen of the Americans.

He then traveled to Sudan in Africa as part of a hunger relief mission. He gently held starving children as doctors examined them. He next flew to India. There, he met with Mother Teresa, who worked to help poor people in India. Ali also visited hospitals and orphanages in India.

In May 1994, he went to Vietnam with the families of U.S. soldiers who'd never returned from the Vietnam War. The families met Vietnamese families whose sons were also missing. Ali thought it was a great thing to see people who had been enemies making peace with each other.

Ali's Message

Muhammad Ali has been called the most beloved and important athlete in history. He is one of the most photographed and most interviewed personalities in the world of sports. He has been the subject of more books and articles than nearly any other athlete. His opponents also got more attention and more money by fighting him than they did by fighting anyone else.

In 1996, the U.S. Olympic Committee chose Ali to light the Olympic flame at the Summer Games in Atlanta. Ali felt honored to light the torch in Martin Luther King Jr.'s hometown. Before Ali left the stadium, U.S. president Bill Clinton told him, "They didn't tell me who would light the flame, but when I saw it was you, I cried." The newspaper *USA Today* named Muhammad Ali "Athlete of the Century" in 1999, and *Sports Illustrated* magazine awarded him a similar honor.

Yet Ali doesn't believe his work is done. In 2000, the U.S. Congress passed the Muhammad Ali Boxing Reform Act. The Ali Act sets up fair guidelines that fighters, promoters, and others must follow. For example, the guidelines help protect fighters from promoters

IT'S A FACT!

At the 1996 Olympic Games, officials gave Ali a second gold medal. It replaced the one he'd thrown in the Ohio River in 1960.

taking too much money or from forcing fighters to sign long-term contracts. The act also sets forth health and safety practices. It establishes standards for ranking boxers.

In 2004, Ali was again in the spotlight. He won the Kahlil Gibran Spirit of Humanity Award for his work in making people aware of world hunger. That same year, the city of Louisville began to build the Muhammad Ali Center as a museum and meeting place. Ali also went to the U.S. Congress. He asked that a U.S. Boxing Commission be set up.

Corruption in Boxing

Corruption, or unfair practices, has long given professional boxing a bad name. Promoters set up fights, so they have a lot of power. Some have taken more money than was outlined in the boxer's contract. Some have forced boxers to sign long-term contracts or to hire a promoter's relative.

Sanctioning organizations—groups that award titles in each weight class—have grown in number. They run independently and set up their own ratings systems. Their ratings sometimes have had more to do with money than with a boxer's skill. Each sanctioning organization wants to promote its "champion," so it ignores top boxers from other sanctioning organizations. As a result, boxing fans have rarely been able to see a bout between opponents of equal skill. The Muhammad Ali Act tries to fix these practices.

In 2001, Will Smith starred as Muhammad Ali in a movie called *Ali*. The movie tells the story of the famous fighter's life.

Ali hopes the commission will help protect fighters further from unfair business practices that hurt them physically and financially.

The Greatest himself concludes: "People say I had a full life, but I ain't dead yet. . . . There's bigger work I got to do. The whole world is in trouble. . . . My main goal now is helping people and preparing for the hereafter."

GLOSSARY

civil rights movement: a group that joined together to push for freedom and equal treatment of all members of society under the law

Communist: a person who supports a government system in which the government owns most property and controls most labor and trade

grade point average: a level of school testing, ranging from A to F. Cassius Clay's average of D-minus is near the bottom of the testing scale.

Islam: a major world religion that began in the Middle East about 1,400 years ago. Followers of Islam are called Muslims. Muslims believe in Allah as God and in Muhammad as his prophet. The religion's holy book is the Quran.

Nation of Islam: a religion founded by Wallace D. Fard and based on the traditional religion of Islam. Like Islam, followers of the Nation of Islam (called Black Muslims) worship Allah as the one true God. Unlike Islam, however, Black Muslims believe that white people are evil and that black people are Allah's favorite.

racial discrimination: an opinion formed unfairly about a racial group. Racial discrimination can lead to racial segregation, or the practice of keeping racial groups apart.

the South: in the United States, the states that fought against the Union (or the North) in the Civil War (1861–1865)

Vietnam War: a conflict that took place from 1954 to 1975 in the present-day Southeast Asian nation of Vietnam

Source Notes

7 Karl Evanzz, *I Am the Greatest: The Best Quotations from Muhammad Ali* (Kansas City, MO: Andrews McMeel Publishing, 2002), vi.

7 Thomas Hauser, *Muhammad Ali: His Life and Times* (New York: Simon & Schuster, 1991), 3.

11 Ibid., 19.

14 David Remnick, *King of the World* (New York: Random House, 1998), 89.

15–16 Ibid.

16 Ibid., 95.

16 José Torres, *Sting like a Bee: The Muhammad Ali Story* (Chicago: McGraw Hill / Contemporary Books, 2001), 77–78.

19–20 Arthur Daly, "Man with a Future," *New York Times*, May 14, 1961.

27 Bud Schulberg, "From Louisville to Liston," *Observer* (London), November 2, 2003, http://observer.guardian.co.uk/osm/story/0,6903,1072708,00.htm (November 18, 2004).

28–29 Torres, 115.

33 Howard L. Bingham and Max Wallace, *Muhammad Ali's Greatest Fight: Cassius Clay vs. the United States of America* (New York: M. Evans and Company, Inc., 2000), 73.

33 Hauser, 71.

34 Robert Cassidy, *Muhammad Ali: The Greatest of All Time* (Lincolnwood, IL: Publications International, Ltd., 1999), 41.

35 Hauser, 78.

35 Audrey Edwards and Gary Wohl, *Muhammad Ali: The People's Champ* (Boston: Little, Brown and Company, 1977), 35.

36 "Muhammad Ali," *Gale Group*, 2004, http://www.galegroup.com/free_resources/bhm/bio/ali_m.htm (December 13, 2004).

39 Hauser, 82–83.

40 Harry Mullan, ed., *The Book of Boxing Quotations* (London: Stanley Paul, 1988), 139.

47 *10K Truth Quotes Muhammad Ali*, 2004, http://www.10ktruth.com/the_quotes/ali.htm (November 9, 2004).

49 Edwards, 14.

50 Don Atyeo and Dennis Felix, *Muhammad Ali: The Glory Years* (New York: Miramax Books, 2003), 128.

52 Bingham and Wallace, 124.

52 "Performer and Cultural Hero," *Africaonline*, n.d., http://www.africaonline.com/ali_hero.htm (November 9, 2004).

56 Ibid.

56 "Simply and Truly 'the Greatest,'" *Courier-Journal*, 2003, http://www.courier-journal.com/2000/soul_ali.html (November 9, 2004).

57 Atyeo and Felix, 170.

57–58 Hauser, 173.

59 Ibid., 181.

59 Ibid., 189.

60 Bingham and Wallace, 190.

61 Hauser, 131.

62 Ibid., 184.

63 Elliot J. Gorn, *Muhammad Ali: The People's Champ* (Chicago: University of Illinois Press, 1995), 146.

66 Mullan, 141.

66 Ibid., 92.

66 Hauser, 221.

66 *Brothers United as One International*, 2002, http://www.brothersonline.com/shadows.html (November 9, 2004).

67 Mullan, 141.

70 Hauser, 234.

74 Ibid., 185.

74 Ibid., 364.

75 Muhammad Ali and Richard Durham, *The Greatest: My Own Story* (New York: Random House, 1975), 29.

75 Gorn, 81–82.

78 Mullan, 124.

80 Hauser, 313.

81 Joe Frazier and Phil Berger, *Smokin' Joe: The Autobiography of a Heavyweight Champion of the World* (New York: Macmillan USA, 1996), 166.

81 *BBC Sport*, March 7, 2001 http://news.bbc.co.uk/sport1/hi/other_sports/1205393.stm (November 9, 2004).

85 "Lawdy, Lawdy, He's Great," *CNN Sports Illustrated*, 1999, http://sportsillustrated.cnn.com/centurys_best/news/1999/05/05/thrilla_manila/ (November 9, 2004).

85 "Still Smokin," *The Australian*, October 2, 2004, http://www.theaustralian.news.com.au/printpage/0,5942,10941006,00.html (November 9, 2004).

87 Stephen Brunt, *Facing Ali: The Opposition Weighs In* (Guilford, CT: Lyon's Press, 2002), 179.

89 Hauser, 353.

93 Ibid., 406–407.

95–96 Ibid., 426.

96 Evanzz, 104.

99 Hauser, 470.

100 Ibid., 474.

100 Mullan, 140.

101 Alex Tresniowski and Kelly Carter, "In His Image," *People Weekly*, April 26, 1999, 103.

101 Ibid.

Selected Bibliography

Ali, Muhammad, and Richard Durham. *Muhammad Ali in His Own Words*. New York: Pinnacle Books, 1975.

Bingham, Howard L. *Muhammad Ali: A Thirty-Year Journey*. New York: Funk & Wagnalls, 1968.

Gelman, Steve. *Young Olympic Champions*. New York: Norton, 1964.

Hauser, Thomas. *Muhammad Ali Memories*. New York: Rizzoli, 1992.

Lewis, Claude. *Cassius Clay: A No-Holds-Barred Biography of Boxing's Most Controversial Champion.* New York: Macfadden-Bartell Corp., 1965.

Mailer, Norman. *The Fight.* Boston: Little, Brown and Company, 1975.

______. *Norman Mailer on the Fight of the Century.* New York: New American Library, 1971.

Nack, William. "Young Cassius Clay." *Sports Illustrated,* January 13, 1992, 70–81.

Olsen, Jack. *Black Is Best: The Riddle of Cassius Clay.* New York: Putnam, 1967.

Pacheco, Ferdie. *Muhammad Ali: A Portrait in Words and Photographs.* New York: Crowell, 1975.

Sugar, Bert Randolph. *The Great Fights: A Pictorial History of Boxing's Greatest Bouts.* New York: Rutledge Press, 1981.

______, ed. *The Ring Record Book and Boxing Encyclopedia.* New York: Atheneum, 1981.

Sullivan, George. *The Cassius Clay Story.* New York: Fleet Publishing Corp., 1964.

Further Reading and Websites

Buckley, James, Jr. *Muhammad Ali.* Circle Pines, MN: World Almanac Library, 2004.

Cebulash, Mel. *Lights Out: Great Fights of the 20th Century.* Syracuse, NY: New Readers Press, 1993.

Freedman, Suzanne. *Clay v. United States: Muhammad Ali Objects to War.* Berkeley Heights, NJ: Enslow Publishers, 1997.

Godron, Randy. *Muhammad Ali.* New York: Grosset & Dunlap, 2001.

Hook, Jason. *Muhammad Ali: The Greatest.* Austin, TX: Raintree, 2001.

International Boxing Hall of Fame
http://www.ibhof.com
The official website of the Hall of Fame in New York provides stories, statistics, photos, and more about the history of boxing.

Knapp, Ron. *Top 10 Heavyweight Boxers.* Berkeley Heights, NJ: Enslow Publishers, 1997.

Latimer, Clay. *Muhammad Ali.* Chanhassen, MN: Child's World, 2000.

Lewis, Jon E. *The Life and Times of Muhammad Ali.* Broomall, PA: Chelsea House, 1997.

Muhammad Ali Center
http://www.alicenter.org
The website of the museum and meeting center devoted to Ali is still being built. It will be a place that will share Ali's ideals, as well as give information about him and his career.

Myers, Walter Dean. *The Greatest: Muhammad Ali.* New York: Scholastic, 2001.

Official Website of Muhammad Ali
http://www.ali.com
Ali's official website includes letters, a way to ask Ali questions, lists of statistics, and more.

Wilmore, Kathy. *Muhammad Ali: With a Discussion of Honesty.* Boston: Learning Challenge, 2003.

INDEX

Photo Acknowledgments

Photographs are used with the permission of: © AP Wide World Photos, pp. 4, 62, 101; © CORBIS, p. 6; © Bettmann/CORBIS, pp. 8, 11, 17, 20, 25, 29, 35, 42, 43, 45, 46, 49, 53, 55, 59, 64, 67, 69, 73, 74, 84, 89, 94, 97; © Keystone/Getty Images, p. 32; © Time Life Pictures/Getty Images, p. 36; © Central Press/Hulton Archive/Getty Images, p. 47; © DPA/EMPICS/DPA, p. 79; © Lynn Goldsmith/CORBIS, p. 86; © Frank Tewkesbury/Evening Standard/Getty Images, p. 91; © Scott Gries/Getty Images, p. 99; © Columbia/The Kobal Collection/ Connor, Frank, p. 105.

Cover: © Photofest.